FASTER, ANNIHILATORS!

FASTER, ANNIHILATORS!

Travis Hupp

atmosphere press

AUTHOR'S NOTE

How much can we survive? That question can be broadly applied to most of the poems collected in this volume. Admittedly, you may not find any clear answers. What you *will* find is resilience pulled from despair, a sense of humor in the face of doom, and abiding love that even roiling anger can't obscure.

These poems were written over the last 24 odd years, from just before I started high school in 1996 to January of 2023. They chronicle my journey to accept myself as a gay man and come out of the closet in a time well before gay rights were the law of the land in America, and when anti-LGBTQ+ violence felt like an ever-present threat in my small southern town.

There are poems about descending into drug addiction, dealing with the side-effects, quitting cold turkey, relapsing, and quitting again (as of this writing, I'm in a treatment program, am 5 months clean and feeling strong in my recovery).

There are poems about my struggle with, and inevitable embrace of, what are either auditory hallucinations caused by drug use, a psychic awakening, or a bit of both (and both is the theory I mostly subscribe to, though it depends somewhat on the moment).

There are poems about love found and love lost, love unrequited, and love dangerous and inconvenient to voice. There are poems that rage at the sustained assault on democracy, decency and the biosphere that was the trump administration, and poems that take heart in the "bold blue" progress accomplished during President Obama's time in office. There are poems that take fiery aim at homophobia, racism, sexism and other bigotries alongside poems that detail me wrestling with the implications of being a gay Christian who also reads tarot cards and dabbles in spellcraft (what can I say? There's never been much "traditional" about me, but accepting Jesus made a huge positive impact on me when I was incarcerated and I've felt a strengthened connection to the divine ever since).

One poem that is particularly heartbreaking for me to read, yet profoundly special to me, bears witness to my sweet cat, Sage, and her grieving process after her litter of kittens were all born with fatally under-developed lungs. There's even a poem that nerds out about the current era of X-Men comics and gives Marvel credit for always using the mutant metaphor to stand up for the oppressed and ostracized, and to stand up to bullies and bigots, no matter how large their number or how loudly they hate.

To LGBTQ+ readers, I hope these poems make you feel seen and less lonely. That they help you stoke the anger at persistent injustice you're entitled to, and that you channel that energy into bold action and dynamic art that moves the needle toward equality. I hope the fact that I'm still standing to write this and you're still here to read it reminds you how unbelievably strong the community you're an essential part of is.

And to readers of any orientation, from anywhere, of any background, race or gender identity, whether you love or hate my work, I sincerely thank you for reading. I hope I at least give you something to think about.

I don't know what the limit is to how much we can survive, but we apparently haven't hit it yet. That alone is a reason for celebration and wild, stubborn hope.

CONTENTS

DESPAIR

HOPE

LOVE

HIDING PLACE

I see nothing but black
and red these days
except the gauzy
pink fireworks
going off in my face
when I let my red out
in my black hiding place

OUT OF ORDER

With a whisper of falling cards
the house spirals out of order
Like a false god or a jacket shrugged off
The ill-fitting idea we'd ever be strong

The house spirals out of order
Lovers savage lovers
The ill-fitting idea we'd ever be strong
means it's easy to divide us and kill us one by one

Lovers savage lovers
No such thing as brothers
means it's easy to divide us and kill us one by one
Now we're dying in the dark, we don't remember having loved

No such thing as brothers
Animosity need cower no longer
Now we're dying in the dark, we don't remember having loved
We can't all blame each other, we can't all blame the drugs

Animosity need cower no longer
It unhinges its jaw as it prowls every shadow
We can't all blame each other, we can't all blame the drugs
It doesn't matter where the blame lies; it's after all of us

but now your suppurating
empty narcissism
is gnawing my very identity

CHARM OFFENSIVE

The hypno-rays just emanate
A horny ensorcelling that never abates

It's wrong to work on my heart's hormonal hopes
With hallucinogenic hot hunk honey

A violation! I proclaim
No, wait! God's sake, let's date!

Taking it away would be the more terrible trauma
Going away is the assault on the pit of all concerned innards

Vanish nonchalant with me not consenting
My fury will worry your bespoke bachelor pad down

If you're leaving town
this siren is screaming in surround sound on your shoulder

Under arrest?
Of course you are

By the all-other-authority-invalidating-usurping
of my ardent amorous intentions

You know not of who you speak
yet you speak your premature, uninformed *no*

I absorb it and attend to it
Embrace the no, embody it

I'm no price now
No's the prize now

I'm the short, blessed word
You bestowed on me
No is the love we make, us two
The only shared experience I can cling to or cloak in

So come at me, bro
Flaunt that flighty frat-boy coldness

Offend me when you charm me
with your effortless charm offensive

How you count me not even
as a collateral kill

So I kneel to worship
Devout in my damage

Still ruder than that
are your reductive ranges

You see not that I'm broken
Don't see me as a tired hoebag queen there's just no hope for

You see me not
Sense not my absence

Find formlessness where I form up
friendly and feisty to fascinate you

Maybe that's why my *spare me* sense is tingling
I'll give you your *FUCK NO!* to go

EXPLETIVE COMPLETED

All this constant rainbow puking
revision spinning
strictly g-rated
unstimulating
radio-edited
chin up bullshit
anchors and submerges

There is no up
There is capitalist whoredom
There is the marketing eye
The bargain basement markdown
You settle for level
and marvel at your progress
You cozy up to who you need
You give admiration
in exchange for advancement

There's nothing I can do for you
I'm not above you
I'm just away from you
These are categorically
not rainbows
boiling in my stomach
I don't want to weed out the ugly
I'm not after Sesame Street's audience

I'm not lazy enough for platitudes
Curses are just part of discourse
That expletive deleted

I want completed
and I'm willing to take it
by force

FITFUL

Don't want this.
Thick red evil.
Seep deeper.
Settle safely.
I store it.
Implore it.
My spiral recycles.

Love's fitful.
Dreaming badly.
Cloth to love's brow.
Doting.
Devout.
Seems our good dreams
give each other nightmares.

Sunday best smiles.
Swallowed doubts.
Our own vows.
Cuff links glint.
Our time is now.

Music swelling.
Scalpels out.

ALL I'VE EVER HATED

I want to break in half so I'm harder to kill
Some vital parts of me hidden at any given time
I don't know why it's the cynical side
who never runs for the bunker this year

I want to stop
Shut down and shut off
Drain from myself
Then I want to recharge

I want to be solar powered
until the sun goes down
Then eat all the stars
if there's enough to curb my hunger

I could be one myself
I could scorch this skin right off me
Flash fry these bones
and the brain that makes me needy

and devour myself
if outer space is empty

I want to run out in traffic
crushing any cars that dare to hit me
Turn on the drivers
like they're all I've ever hated

Could I hear "amen!" when I'm angry just once
Not when zealots slam the doors of their churches
on traumatized teens who believe themselves
too much to humor an ignorant preacher

I want to disperse my molecules
Endowing each with at least five senses
Send them out as satellites
dividing further into atoms
I want to amputate my fingers
so I can't hold a cigarette
Tear out someone's heart
and hit my stopwatch when they notice it

Can I keep making all these efforts
as I'm chewed and digested by hunger

GAVEL HAND

Time may fly but
if you try you'll die
Not a lift-off limb on you
or on me for that matter

Not enough on the total summed from
humanity's collective endeavors

At best we're damaged goods
Not born dead or *just* damaged
Apparently, some never even
get gifted the goods to start with

If I get inklings who's who
I'm still withholding judgment
I'm not a man who assumes
My gavel hand
can always be trusted

But should faith in even God's
be unskeptically unfettered
Worshippers are making moves
Well word up
but are they manic or magic
Who is really the shit
Most of us seem like
another near miss

Transcendence
Cognizance
Hedonism
Psionic karate kicks
All can fail
All will flail

Especially Justice
The twisted old rapist

HUDDLED MADNESS

*"Give me your tired... your poor
Your huddled masses... because I'm hungry"*

My people also
scraped hulls on these shores
My people too
in the same boats with yours

They adorned their necks
with the crucifix
longing to be good
witless Christians

They dreamt about
your moral high ground
Never dreaming it would be
their bones you climbed to reach it

FASTER, ANNIHILATORS!

Who can tell how anything feels anymore?
How can I tell if I feel anymore?
I think I'm numb to my hurt's immensity.
Desensitized to most of me.

The doctor scowls 'cos I shouldn't be smiling.

Perhaps I'm barking mad.
The neighbor's dog is barking.
I begin to understand.
Barking mad at the heavy chain.
Barking mad at the strangling collar.
Pacing a yard he swears gets smaller.
He and I commiserate.
My neighbor, naturally, is widely loved.

He's bereft and barking immoral.

The world beyond our tethers,
unmicrocosmed (or otherwise microcosmed)
It's all crude oil cowboys.
All tech-savvy trendsetting hipstermancers.
All gun blast and gut spray.
Arterial bleeding.
Thick rain of brain matter.

What do I know of it, really?
What they tell me, mostly.
Who was I, if anyone, yesterday?
Why can't I remember who knows me?
Answer faster, annihilators!
Repudiate my reason, breeders!

Where but destruction are you leading?

Should we spend more time deciding on drive-thru
or thinking about who should be president?
Faster. Faster.
Feed our despondence.

Fast food is life is politics.

Faster, slo-mo bastards.
Faster, bangers of innocence.
Republican rutters on power thrusters.
Faster, annihilators!
Faster, oblivion!
Make me feel it all,
then none of it.

I only climax to apocalypse.

YOUR ENTIRE REGIME

Somewhere between jack eight and
jack eighteen and a half
while my past assailed me
with things I forgot to avenge
after a spell of almost blindness
I almost tore up my poems
A chronicle of almosts
Almost fatal almost loves

It seems characteristic of straight folks
to confuse euphoric with weightless
Do you know what weightlessness feels like?
It's not the release you imagine
It's a role you thrust on the rest of us
and we never wanted to play it

You don't get to regulate us
to an almost non-existence

For instance
imagine you're living your life
Almost always polite
Minding your business
Then some idiot
draws a knife, a revolver
You know, typical villain shit
And you can drift off
protecting yourself
but not the other innocents
Because you can't stop assailants
without any weight
to tackle with

Just know this isn't what I wanted
To be blurting bitter messages
In fact
I hunted inspiration
to help me write anything
other than this

I stalked it in old pictures
We were in them
We were faded
Even that inspired this
Faded
Too close to weightless

Still
That's almost camaraderie, right?
That we were
All of us
Faded?
Tell me
If I flip through the pictures again
Will I be the only one in them?

Somewhere between calling me
"faggot" and "queer"
while you leaned so easy on the rail
After grasping the rail
to not feel weightless
I banished your voice altogether

I banished a voice I'd grown to love
Never questioning why I loved it

Camaraderie
was always enough for me
The voice offered nothing
but mockery

I don't know who you think you are
But I'm not
and you're not
what you think
and since your voice
is one of many
I banish your entire regime

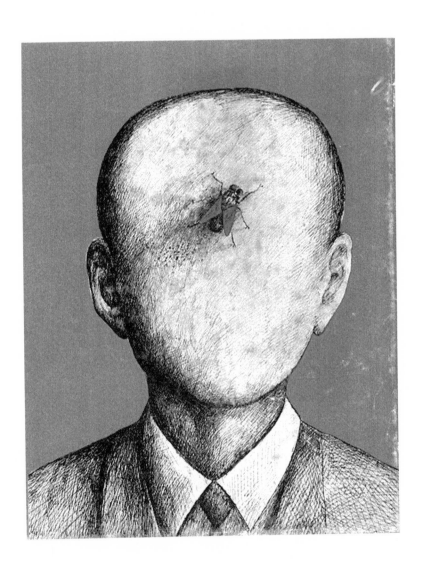

FACE TOWARD

Start, stop. Stop and start.
Be not bitter, Twitter tart.
There's much media to manage you.
Social. Visual. Virtual. Audio. Unstoppable.
Interactive HD porno.

Brandished boners of benevolence.
VD vindictive. Itch of inciting insight.
In everyone's core is something insidious.
Dormant, perhaps, 'til a reckless word summons it.

Fall into the offered embrace. By fracking and fire
your edifice defaced. Journey darkly. Pace in place.
Cere-be-bellum st-stuttering in unguttering hidden shame
'til your throat screams you blind and your eyes
face toward brain.

Stay. Go away. Stay away. Go awry.
Go rogue. Rouge Bumfucksburg.
Rag the storied riches. Rig the supplicant systems.
Supplant the stymied citizens.

Investigate erroneously. Err on the side of ennui.
Turn back the full force of pummeling tides
with your churning, misplaced pride.
It's hell on moral right, but easy on the spine.

Sleepwalk daylight drudgery. Daydream dawning night.
Dawdle before yawning downfall. Fate's mottled maw.
Your meat wolfed raw. Spoils spoiled. Saviors severed.

Middling beginnings ended. Boring battle scars.
Friends unfriended. Climax canceled. Shrouds shrugging skyward.
Souls shrieking, shriveled, southbound. Little loser lost's
disappointing destiny found. Mangled polls and mangled poles.
Flaccid from famine, Earth goes flat all around.
The alt-right, for once, rendered right. The left swears vengeance
and surrenders on sight. President Boss Baby bombs bad
and not briefly. A treasonous, tragic comedy. Broadcast intergalactically.

LAIR

We will fail to protect you.

Once you're fertilizer, we'll rob your families.

In our boundless cruelty, we'll let you expose our collective, cesspool heart.

You will appear on news shows and we will watch you.

We'll hear your allotted thirty seconds.

Some ludicrous garbage about how our crimes against you must stop.

Maybe we'll smile, knowing it makes you feel powerless.

That we have legions of faces.

That every single one of us can blame someone else.

Your rallying cries will be written off as begging.

We're fortunate you're slow to realize your faces outnumber even ours.

If you wanted to untangle the snaking wires of our corruption, we couldn't do much to stop you.

If you wanted to replace us, we would be replaced.

And still we dare abuse you.

Insult you.

Lie to you.

Incur your wrath.

We really have little control of ourselves.

We plugged into this machine.

Now the machine is all there is.

The machine is all we'll permit.

Those of us fighting our programming have moments of lucidity.

We don't admit it often, but we know we must be stopped.

Not stopped by propaganda fanatics.

Stopped by you, our power source.

You must not settle for soundbites.

Confront us in our lair.

X MARKS

Stalwart and upright against extinction level events
Not too dizzy for data backups so the atomized can mend
Once we re-exist, we'll re-enlist
Just euthanize the patient to cure their slipped disc

Nerd culture is the hippest mainstream craze
Someone learning Krakoan just told a Mexican
to go back to Spain
X marks the overt metaphor for cultural oppression
New converts X that subtext out and look at the pretty explosions

Those are LGBTQ friendly explosions
I bet that inspires some latent emotions

I can't remember anyone the writers have forgotten
as I'm immersed in the mutagenic opera
I want to be fully redeemed and still striving
I want to never falter
To only have the flesh be weak
in service to the right subplot

FREE TO OBEY

10,000 requirements to meet
before we've any interest in meeting you
Fresh air fouled with unironic exceptionalism
You can be one of us
The brave bullying bigly
The God-favored fucking fully FREE!!!

Just renounce your morality
Cut out the curious
Cling to what cowers
Remember knowing and caring is for fags
You're not free to fag out willy nilly
Not in this free country
Not happening
No hoped for happiness
Not for heretics
Not by accident nor happenstance

You are free to become dust
Free to fawn over or fight corporate ambivalence
Free to go to jail
If you're perceptive
If you're drunk
If you breathe a truth to liars in blue

Whatever you would choose for yourself
the result would be a cell
You simply lack the work ethic
You lack the mental health

What kind of compassionate
starsy-barsy free country would we be
if we let living the life you want
be an option for just anybody

You're free to flatter the founding fathers
That's what we mean by freedom
You're free to obey every American ghost
who was even a footnote

Because you are not even a footnote
"Nowhere, None!" we'd say
if we told you where to go

You're free to do everything anyone says
if they're American and dead
or anti-American and rich
What the fuck do you mean that's not
what patriotism is

Just follow the *PEW-PEW-BANG-BANG-BLAM!!!*
That most American soundtrack
Bleed your subpar blood
Be healed, sick sinner
Blankly thank us
Be polite, whoever you were
Whatever you thought we'd let you be

Let your betters concentrate
Be quiet like you've been taught
before our focus slips
and you form independent thoughts

LOUD

One such as me
must know when to be loud
There's much to be changed here
Many houses to be screamed down
Houses are good, important things
except when they're situated
on top of you
and through the floorboards
you're always hearing
they still don't think
they've hidden you well enough

RELIGION, MYSTICISM & THE METAPHYSICAL

PAINTED CORNER

Painted in a corner's fine
as long as it's in mine

Such a spirited old soul should not
believe in only science

The mad maestro in the basement
is losing concentration

His housemates sleep above him
He hopes one day to awaken

Awaken them as he awakens himself
to the beauty of the painted corner

Everyone chooses their trappings
but his loneliness isn't mournful

All science was once thought magic
Once everyone was primitive

Spells and prayers and experiments
Each of them has rituals

Efforts to explore them
can border on identical

You can throw numbers at anything
and confuse it into submission

Love doesn't fit your figures
You can't appraise your intuition

Its value can't be totaled
The source of it is no one's to question

It's deeper than the heart of you
Higher than any resplendent Heaven

No scalpel or probe can penetrate it
No Bible or scroll can minister it from existence

There are too many angles to view it from
for any single discipline to explain it

We can only define it together
Only by disagreement

SIJOS FOR A BLOOD MOON

If there is no proof it must be true, wouldn't you say?

If you cuss nothing's curse and nothing responds, ask it for
its name.

Blood moon howls and witching hours at twelve or is it three?

Annoyed equally by droning voices and actual drones.

Announcers dodge composite bouncers and shriek "send in
the clones!"

Skywritten circles and nosedives hurtful for equanimity.

If you catch the villain does it mean you are heroic?

Will you still be martyred if you are stubbornly stoic?

Rhetorical questions answered by demonic activity.

Does God remember our names, does God remember His own?

Do mortals only earn straitjackets trying to earn a throne?

Starvation seems to be favored by Heaven over gluttony.

Avenged ineptly by hosts of resplendent better angels.

Prowlers impersonate allies, cheaters run the tables.

Father, Son and Holy Ghost bring the karmic rule of infinity.

SERPENTINE

We were branches
of a body of water
Our currents could be impeded
but they were undeniably connected

That was before the world ended

We still debate
exactly what happened
as if the madness was alien to us
when in fact we *were* the madness

We were always efficient killers
but this I couldn't have fathomed

We burned enemies and their families
Then tried to re-light the ashes
Now we're as dead as they are
'cos we're nothing but our damage

Now we beg for water
Beg for what composes us
Scrape our sandpaper tongues
down the length of a ravine's
serpentine carcass

and I taste no connection
Not if I'm honest

RAP SHEET

Think I'm on the fritz or in on the fix.
Don't forget the first rule of I.T.
Turn me off if you can, your casual majesty.
So kind to invite peasants to the pageant.
If my dreams be damned, do your damndest.

Do you ever think you might be the devil?
Why did I ask you a question so evil?

Think you're genuflecting and genuinely freaked.
Don't judge all of me by my internet rap sheet.
Turn you on if I can, you're above all that.
Why don't you taste aloof, isn't proof in your pudding?
I resent my ravenous swallows and gulping.

Can I ever get a win by right of karma?
Dressed as a far-fetched dues ex machina?

Think we're overdressed and underthinking
how power thinks better of staying uncoupled.
Word to the rising, *so* homo, hot mofo.
Hapless my incantations, incandescent he strutted.
0 Fool most beloved, from the Tower defenestrated.

What delicate flavors of pinwheeling divinity?
Is the psychic sky just one angry entity?

NEFARIOUS FIRE

Who am I to know what's right for me?
How could I think I know me best?
Where do I get off having other thoughts
besides *repentrepentrepent?*

Who are we that we give kids nightmares?
Program them young with threat of nefarious fire
in which souls boil over and demons conspire?
Yet we swear all the while
there's no such thing as monsters

So there is a Hell, or there isn't a Hell.
Either way, we're liars.

A DREAM I HAD

Sterilized afterlife, lab coat angels

Like army recruiters, working their angles

It all made sense, it was very well ordered

Heaven expanding, stretching its borders

Now I'm on Earth again, where we all have our limits

Planting seeds on a planet the meek are due to inherit

Spend too much time expecting Hell, though, paradise will look
just like it

No need to bust your stitches if you can't swear off your vices

Deepening Heaven on the make

We are its devices

No fear of early graves

We don't remain inside them

No textbooks lying open there

Just instruments a-gleam, ever polished

Test tubes, ageless embryos

Cocooned, not yet incarnate

We're given this experiment

Let's stop experimenting with carnage

Don't turn down the volume

before the music's even started

THE MIDDLE DISTANCE

Hallucinations or real events
Psychic awakening or screaming
from the middle distance
where the woods sprawl
from foreground to periphery

Can't see the victims for the forest
or the victimizers for the trees

Maybe identities mean less these days
Maybe the howls are all just me;
My breakdown's latest phase

Maybe I'm going schitz…
sc…sc…schitzofrenetic
That's what the fuck I call it
No matter how you define it
or your verbiage confines it

Visitors at my door or invaders
in my brain stem
Numbering the eyes I
can use to see them

Now that their hypnotic
tenor and bass
resounds like echolocation
Re-verves like nobody's business
but mine
Reroutes my predestination

DECEIVERS

Deceivers patrol perimeters
Punishments administered
All around and inside you
In staccato discordance

"Drip drip drip"
Say festering threats
"Abandon yourself"
"Accept your abandonment"

A bad seed planted
Under a bad sign, bent
Against an ill wind
of apocalyptic portent

In love or in luck
this one's important

NOT ENOUGH INK

Some rinky-dink revelation

I can't explain

There's not enough ink

Again I blink

Again I change

Something just shifted

A dying fire rekindled

A ghost stepping through me

It leaves; rejoins the mist

but it left something with me

Skin me with gentle scalpels

and tell me what it is

Why these withered secrets

on lips that want a kiss

Even my pen only harvests fractured bits

Puzzle pieces scattered

kicked into corners

Some beneath the rug

All the rest disjointed

All these things I think I know

All these pages trying to excavate them

Maybe they're mine alone

All inside

All in codes

Codes of honor ruling out codes of conduct

There's not enough ink

in this world or the next one

Again I get a glimpse

of clear reception that slips into static

Again I taste fickle freedom

Why can't I lose my baggage

Drug me like the doctors have

Tell me how I'm improving

How I'm getting stronger from

everything I'm losing

I don't believe it anymore

I swallow the pills my stomach wants to reject

I itch

I twitch

My guts learn how to braid

I think this medicine is all that afflicts me now

I think I'm entitled to my depression

I think somewhere in it

Someone chained up some secrets

and I can't position the puzzle

without access to those pieces

ALARMIST

Input pinned, solicited sins
Beckon calls, feckless brawls
A shell of static, a cocoon of sadness
A warrior unmoved, a weapon to woo

Start making sense soon
Stop breaking 3 am's doom
If you ever understand a damn thing
Hear what I say and feel what it means

Means to ends, stilts and springs
Crème de la crème, any contraption to reach
A little on the nose, a whistle for assistance
Unchoose what I chose, a bit of embarrassment

Stop taking sickness seriously
Start faking miraculous recovery
If you detect threats, vicious, bodiless
Track back the attacks
Step silent, alarmist

REGARDS

Whatever pronouns you use
They're real
Everyone's heard of
the God of Israel

His name is bandied about everywhere
Sometimes even for the right reasons
I pray to sustain gladness in Her
through the sadness of mortal seasons

God, do not abandon me
God, do not forget
I make mistakes but I'm not just mistakes
I'm getting better
Please give me Your best

HYPOCRITE'S NOTEBOOK

I dream all the time

I dream of being authentic

while writing in an *American Scholar* notebook

I've never been much of a scholar

and often curse my country

Yet I use the notebook's paper

What a goddamn phony

WORLDS AWAY

Numbness. Nothingness.
Near total isolation.
Pride. The fall.
Broken by cravings.
Amphetamines. Reefer.
Getting laid. Making love.
Coffee. Entertainment.
Revolution. Rock and roll.

Depression. Desolation.
Sudden rapid entropy.
Blank. Sharp. Everywhere.
Angels without mercy.
Frigid greetings. Steel touches.
Glimpses of former softness.
Interruptions. Undoings.
The loss of all permanence.

Failure. Futility.
A dark day's eternal dawn.
Rebounds. Revelations.
Useless. Dead wrong.
Hope in defiant strands.
Carried aloft. Led astray.
Impertinence of no importance.
Voices from worlds away.

SAGE

Four lights
switched off in three nights
Went out too soon
Never got to be bright

A devoted mother
Did everything right
Thinks it's her fault
the steel came to their eyes

In the end they couldn't breathe
Leaving momma too stunned to grieve
She hunted their spirits
in cabinets and trees

Until the clench of shock lessened
She remembered her babies stiffened
Her eyes ask the question
Why don't I deserve them?

Now they're buried
with seeds
to sprout colors in spring
Put scent in the wind
Give succor to bees

But momma's still shattered
She finds no solace in plants
Her world's been taken
She just wants it back

AN OBJECT IN MOTION

A door, untouched
swings itself shut

The house isn't haunted
Slightly slanted
The only ghosts
gusts and inertia

An object in motion
stays in motion
until it accepts
a lack of all purpose

I haven't accepted it
Energizer Struggle Rabbit
Intermittently rabid
Stumbling over my calculated risks

A fool in motion
stays in motion
until he slits his wrists

Never failing to fuck up the math
Fumble my phrases
Live for your form

Maybe I'm a negative number
A figment faggot's
subtracted fragments

An unsolved fraction
A space-sucking void

Maybe I'm ghosted
Maybe I shut the door

WANT FOR NOTHING

I don't want to want anything
I need to want for nothing
I don't want to need to feel because
it always leads to screaming
Maybe I need my scream to echo
Maybe I should stop fighting my scream
I don't know how much I should fight anymore
I can't fight everything

ANTI-POEM

This is a poem to say
I no longer write poems

An anti-poem

A pre-publication retirement notice

Unless it comes from a place of light
I won't let it out at all
I won't go vigilante with my art
I'm miscast in the hero's part

Again and again it all crashes down

None of it ever my fault

No
I know I have problems
I know I am a problem
More poems would just make more problems

So this is a poem to say
I no longer write poems
I've warned my muse to leave me alone

No verse

No verve

Nobody home

DRESSED

All dressed down with nowhere to go
All spun out with no one to blow
Good God, a gay incel, how fucking hilarious
Except that it isn't and your hyena laugh is heinous
All I got planned is categorizing manias

You're owned by OCD, I'm pulverized by PTSD
We both got ADHD and that's our ABCs
Bad shit, hellish hoodoo, can't fucking shake this
Even if we do, it'll haul hoof to chase us
You and I aghast because we're both betrayers

FOR THE FAITHLESS

You'll know they're wrong
They won't believe you
Death will be an annoyance
Death will not quite kill you

You'll have to keep writing to count them
Those subtle, rattling deaths
One day you'll be glad you had them
if you start to live again

They'll hurt you
whether or not you deserve it
They'll sneer if you get scared
As if there's nothing to be afraid of
in a world of vacant stares

You'll have to keep writing to count them
The things you're not supposed to feel
until you have someone's say so
But feel them you will

You'll love them when you want to hate them
because of details you'll remember
You'll be wary when you try to be reckless
because changes are forever

You'll have to keep writing to count them
The dignified things distorted
You'll get nowhere when you fight it
Knocked out when you ignore it

You'll reach out and lose a hand
You'll try to reattach it
You'll be the first to name their virtues
and discover you imagined them

You'll have to keep writing to count them
Your other, angrier faces
Filling pages, purging poisons
to be good company for the faithless

DIE TRYING

Now that my body demands rest
Now that I must have it
Who are you to judge me?
Who are you, just freshly waking?

I think for a while
it'll all survive without me
I was solemn in vigil yesterday
Awful sorry you missed it

My efforts are no less real for that
Eyelids no less heavy
Raw nerves no less ravaged
Cauterized at the endings

I can't make you see a goddamn thing
No matter how I press, nothing impresses upon you
I'm reasonably certain by now you think
I wake and sleep to spite you
That I'm failing in some sacrosanct duty
because I tried, but never died

You wanna close the book on me, don't you?
You wish I'd just die trying

Do I apologize for not appeasing you?
Sacrifice my heart to your ego?
What exactly do you want from me?
Be specific, name an organ

SKY FULL OF VAPORS

Grating on bone, gears of this machine
bent out of form, other gears compensate

Stirring below despair's debris

Sensing a storm, I wait 'til it abates
to rise from the slate
to face a sky full of vapors
spewed from steaming craters

Lava burns through the fools
Then the lava cools
leaving a sky full of vapors
but nothing for a muse

CUT A DEAL

Light doesn't light
Warmth doesn't warm
I am not myself
The sun is not the sun

I don't know what orbits here
I don't know what I am
I don't know what I orbit
I don't know this system

Adventure's no adventure
Fun isn't much fun
Danger isn't dangerous
because I want this to be done

I want to be over
To enter no more orbits
See no more new seasons
Knock no one else off balance

I want to be off my rocker
This medicine isn't helping
To benefit themselves is why
doctors prescribe my prescriptions

I want my buy out
like the ones the doctors get
Their big moral buy out
to inflate a certain drug's benefits

I need to cut a deal here
so I'll try to live for ten more minutes
I'll try to be fully alive for once
but kill me when it's over with

DISCRETION

Up in vapor, curling smoke
Sometimes I get high when I imbibe
Prod for a response, but you ain't gotta poke

Don't tempt fate in plain sight, curtains conceal
Please use discretion for compartmentalization
All kinds of people got eyesight, myopia is real

Don't dick me over about if I'm getting dicked deep
Exaggeration's no crime, the line's drawn at lying
If it's just you excited, uppers make me sleep

Gravities or blunts, details I don't sweat
It goes to the same place, I call it my face
Just 'cos I'm bored don't mean I'm upset

PLUMMETING

This hour is sour
I'm right in assuming
All words mean burdens
You in your jagged softness
Me scrabbling to map your path
over pantheons of dead toppled tree gods
among sons daughters fathers mothers families
which are not

Kill for a cure for delirium for comfort
which does not
eat away the stomach lining or fossilize
the heart
Bursting so no I can't
find it in me to sing your praises
There is nothing so much nothing the poems
should stay blank pages

The sound all around
you won't hear anywhere
is ancestral pebbles dropped
Plummeting
Plummeting
Plummeting
impacting nothing at all

LIKE IT MATTERS

Like it even matters
what we've done
deserved or borrowed
Whether we've completely
paid our dues
down to every technicality
Whether we always
told the truth
or forgot to tell
the agreed upon lies
Whether we sang or wrote
If we could play or
if we could fight
If we could stomach whatever
they could fit
on their shovels
Whether we spat
in their faces
or kissed their erections
Like it matters who stayed
or who died or who left
or how much we cared
when fate simply didn't
Whether hearts get broken
or fixed when they're failing
or transplanted
to patients
who can't understand
a damn thing they inherit
Whether we say "damn"

or "damnable" or "fuck"
or condescend and speak
to our peers in baby talk
Like it matters if the world dies
in one orgasmic drunken crash
Like we have anything to depend on
if life depends on us
to save its ass

COLLAPSED

Creek water laps
at the boulder where I collapsed
Unburdens a bit by transfer of cold
nothing made to move
could shoulder alone

So easy to lay any old thing
on a surface of unyielding stone

Each day I strive to soften
but my innocence won't show

WELL

You've wished me well since first we met

were always accessible as a friend

I see you on my porch but I will not let you in

I see you and you see me seeing

so I know you know I see you

I will not let you in and I don't care if it hurts you

It isn't that you've wronged me

It's just that you don't matter

I do not wish you well because I do not think about you

I'm not thinking about you now

although I see you filling my window

as I recline on a couch which means more to me than you do

A CHOICE

Dusted again with the grit of goodbyes
stuck in my craw, eyes seeing back in time

Another day of torturous crawl
Night is a symphony, performs one wistful song

Make a choice
Affliction or medication

Make a choice
Oblivion or oblivion

Pray for some light to slice up the shadows
Bitter anger is the answer, it burns ever brighter

Stand and be counted
Categorized, shelved

Line up single file
or stray and be jailed

If you're heartsick
don't say it

If you love
don't mention names

If it's insignificant
cherish it

If it matters
run away

If they fear you
be resigned to it

If they're ignorant
don't teach

If it's cheap
invest freely

If it's proven
don't believe

TIMID BREED

Answers are a timid breed
They shy away from paper
While doubts are born for spotlights
Playing to the audience
and questioning the pleasure

FORTRESS

Can't see out but
I can see in
Feel my way by intuition
It won't be that bad
even though it hurts way too much
I choose belief
I'll just have to toughen up

No clocks in this fortress
that protects the world
from my wounded heart
Once branded a criminal
time means nothing at all
You just get wrung out
trying to wash the stain off
Still I choose wild hope
in the face of creeping torture

They captured an artist
but they paint the wrong portrait

AGILITY

Swing the gates open
for more than animosity
fanned to that same old inferno
burning deeper than third degree
The gauze of the written word
The salve of my own devising
is enough to start the healing

Forcing out gathered shrapnel
with every movement
Stretching senses beyond
physical limitations
Trying to hear
a multiverse singing
Listening with
my own sense of feeling
Exploring and recording
in gossamer hours
when I know
just what it means

Triggers may be pulled
Scattershot may hit me
Because I want to be
a messenger
I preclude my own agility
To speak to guns
like microphones
Empowered by threats to
me and my own
Moved by the beauty of bloody

FROM THE DEPTHS

My love, now it rises
from the depths I did consign it
Not willingly; never willingly
Just by aversion of eyes

By believing in a need for
heavy artillery
when a soft touch was called for
to open shells carefully

When at last tomorrow manifests
When I truly crack
dropped on rocks
it's actually relaxing
to find my casing broken off

So I cut through the wind that
plays me like a violin
without any drive to write
a poem called "Thicker Skin"

My lost, now I find them
as they were before I denied them
They may fail me, may even betray me
Perhaps not with intent
Surely not with every breath

When this abyss widely gapes
a panic follows to escape
I too forget my knowledge

Fail, even betray
I've learned the more you care
the easier it is to make mistakes

My luck, now I change it
Hammer and nail it
I still have all the aches
Won't pretend they're
easy to take
Won't pretend to not
feel grateful
for who I'm still here with
to ache

When at last a clock ticks
away this life's final seconds
and I'm there beside it
thinking it odd it sounds so distant
I'll stretch before the rest
that hovers
amputated from time
and give myself back
with satisfied pride

WARRING FORCES

I've never learned how to make a feeling go away

Never

Not a one

I just collect them

Marveling at how high they can stack

How thinly be filed

How tightly compressed

How they become outmoded before I can even accept their presence

I've never gotten over anything

I've only gone without

I've abstained and maintained a façade of root change

And my reward is mostly Heavenly

Or there's mostly no reward

I've never gotten over cynicism

Never given up optimism

Never equalized warring forces

When I dream of peace now it is only acquiescence

Submitting for bronzing

A lament, laminated

It breaks me and it builds me

It's enraging and enrapturing

EVERY BLESSING

My friends, this poem's an essay
making a case for unflinching clarity.
We're all just trying to be somebody
in a world where only some bodies
are considered anybody.

In this predicament of identity
the brightest brain can become ceremonial.
Our neurological gravitas
hasn't nearly the grit for this.

Our cerebellums posture, powerless.
As fearsome as Queen Elizabeth.
Waving a gloved hand, throwing out a pitch,
so we can pretend that somehow
makes sense of this.

Logic, illogically, prides itself
on being an authority.
Yet logical deduction says
authority is suspected more than trusted.

Logic is the moat yawning wider
'til there's no ground to build a castle on.

Logic is always a hospital.
A hospital bed.
A vaccination.
A plaintive, painful placebo
for a soul's unsterile doctrine.

Do you know why you know you're stricken?
Why you know so intimately what you're stricken with?
It's logic, flouncing about behind the scenes.
Doing nothing of note right now
but naming every illness.

My friends, you'll probably know
a blessing when you see it.
You can tell because the enjoyment of it
is somewhat hindered by reason.

My friends, for every blessing,
there's a zealot to call it a symptom.

It hit me one day
in an avalanche of obviousness
that we got our knowledge of knowledge reversed.
Logic is a luxury but it's simply not very smart.

It chooses the clinic in lieu of the meadow.
Replaces the robust "I must!"
with the monotone echo "I can't."

The moment we make introductions
logic looms with threat of parting.
We're too heavy for the sky
because common sense is on our backs.

NEEDLE THROUGH

I'm not the type to give up on people
so don't make me give you up
You might think I haven't lost too many
I think even one is too much

We could travel all the continents
when we're all rich enough someday
Unravel all our layers and
not scare our whole family away

I try to be above it but
it's sprung and shut so fast
Always where I least expect
the teeth of steel traps

We could free all our limbs
Shake out all the pains
that should've stopped when
we stopped growing
but needle through us all the same

COMMA HOARDER

Kinds of things that alter perception
are friends having faith
or sudden heart failure

Maybe a recipe for soup
you can be poor and still afford

Whittling down your vices
Telling off your boss

Or your mother
gracefully dying
Some uncles
Classmates
Your favorite cousin

After a lot of dying
hallucinations are common

Philosophy is my friend now
Epicurus is my friend
Curl my soul's toenails arrogance
and your homework are my friends

You use too many commas
Abuse your brackets
"Wall it off" says you
"Box it in"

You are too many things to me
I hoard your spare commas
and burn through their legions

Because kinds of things that alter perception
are the long limp from the fire lick
or beer pong in a haunted basement

Everything we're too old for
before getting the hang of being young

Dreams under duress, defying death
A grammatically incorrect thug

THE VOICE WILL KEEP RETURNING

A voice does no good
full volume into the breech
of negative space unheeding
Now I'm suddenly granted a platform
I hope I've a rasp left for any audience

I'd *like* to say:
This is simply who I am
and I'm just a nobody
as representative of everybody
as anybody else

And:
You don't know how it feels
to make sounds in places soundproofed

I've cleared my throat approximately
five hundred times since morning
Straining against a constricting trachea
Not meant to breathe indifference
or the air's more hostile elements

My truth may not be your truth
but it's the only truth that fuels me
and I see now that it isn't so much
that it's hard to understand me
It's hard to just admit
you have it *in you* to understand me
without seeing images of a carpenter
your people say built the world against me

That's what some people say
but the carpenter tells me different

The sounds are on my tongue
as my vocabulary's reconnecting
Some things are said
for no purpose
No benefit
besides the entitlement to shed them

When I love, I'm proud of loving
My regard isn't just for anatomy
I'm not led around by hard-ons
But by the interweaving sinews
of something within me
around me
and more than me

And the dam that holds the words back
might be broken unless it opens
to release mounting pressure
that froths with pent up steam

So the voice will keep returning
despite the air that keeps thinning
The words will keep slipping
and I can't promise I'll try to catch them
because no one has that many aquariums

The sinews will keep stretching outward
Upward, then downward
Coursing through roots and filaments
that riot to feel them

And if that makes me a devil
Hell must be purest Heaven

My truth will keep fueling me
and I'll keep refueling willingly
as I keep understanding
that you might keep *choosing*
to misinterpret me

I'll never finish talking
to myself or to you
'til it stops feeling the same most times
as talking to high strangers

I'll fashion words into olive branches
or, if called for, into razors

Yes, I will fashion words
to do the work of polygraphs
Separate my dawgs
from the vaguely canine sewer rats
Committing to memory
every spike and honest line

Words are all they've allowed me
but not all I'll allow myself

BOLD BLUE

It's an exciting time to be alive
No one has disposable income
except the elite
who are largely disposable
But the upheaval is graphed
in such bold blue directions
It's free to observe
and sometimes to join in
The storyline telegraphed
with a fine poetic justice
Sometimes I must remind myself
And sometimes
to move the plot along
I must remember to forget

MEMORY OF SIGHT

Love larger than a life
I'm living a bit too small

From the ashes of inaction
A pulse in steady waves
Strobing and strong
Navigating ambient energies
around boundaries
mythical from the start

Carbon monoxide consumed for the sake
of more benevolent traits
aching for some space
Yes I have my temples
My sacred grounds, my chants
Garbled, as through tunnels
But where acoustics may fall short
Anything that scrawls, a viable avenue
A harbored hope the words won't distort

If you can't pull away the wicked wool that suffocates
That does much more than hinder eyes
Sometimes when you're blue-faced and blind
you can breathe by twisting your head to one side
and keep on working from the memory of sight

There are legalities, technicalities
There are blueprints, there are plans
Disappointments, disillusionments
Losing the will and getting it back

I'm saying my soul
got snagged somewhere
For a time I hung suspended
I'm saying my love
tripped a deadfall somewhere
Fell dead to the pit of my stomach
Even in the midst of burying it
I tried to give it when it was needed

So listen, because I must clear this up
Grace is not a height
You cannot truly fall from it
if faith catches you when you try

It's something found when
you fear you've lost yours
Something I know because I died
and mine would not let go of me
Whispered *just wait, just write*

So I obeyed
Started writing my death down
and realized one day
I was writing new life

THE ARMORY

Smile like people who know secrets do
Like mysteries ain't no mystery to you

I'm sure you think
you've got me all figured out
You dare not dream me opaque
The truth is
you'll never figure me out
Not in a day
Not in a decade

You can be a blade and
I can smooth your cutting edge
Just when you decide I'm a pacifist
you'll stumble on the armory
I hide in my shed
Just when you think I'm planning
blitzkriegs in my head
you'll look closer at the guns
and find their barrels bent
Triggers rusted motionless
Gunpowder wet

So you will think me defenseless
You'll think me defenseless
as long as I let you

You will think me defective
if I seem to have more sides than you

But though I occasionally malfunction
my dysfunction serves a purpose
The more I fuck up
the more I mean well
The more I fail
the more I'm determined

I have seen what I can do
I can move you to tears
as easily as to war

But if you found one armory
what makes you think I don't have more

RELAPSE EXPECTED

Just maintain
Abide, don't get snide
Abide what you can't
'cos it's better than dying

Better than cracking up
or breaking down while vultures circle
Orbiting tighter, awaiting collapse
Just keep biting back
what you know is eventual

The relapse expected of you
The failure your friends are betting on

Or else fight back
find ways even on your worst days
to put the stars back in your eyes
Assume a battle stance
Bring back mettle to your will

Smile at liars
flashing kindness that kills

BROADCAST TOWER

I find reflections of everything in all of it

Ropes of exhaled smoke

Eyes climb diligent to higher levels

Fortified by drag after drag

Drags me from the body that much faster

Split sidewalk shows me honesty

We take the convenient route even when it's far from perfect

Someone cries out

Cuts it short

Shuts their mouth

Another broadcast tower relaying its love and anguish

Muffled too soon to be sure I even heard it

Building across the street

Vines that try to hide it

Like the you and me we try to be

Pretending it's us growing when things are growing around us

I loosen my grip on all of it

Try not to conjure the ropes quite as often

My eyes can climb up other things
Or rest for a time on someone's best regions

A sidewalk is just a sidewalk

Not every chalk message is meant for me

Still sooner or later

With tower upon tower

One or two will broadcast my frequency

The vines don't conceal what's real

They just make it apparent from a distance

That there are certain embraces

You're trapped in if you get wrapped in

HELL OF A WRECK

My brain recycles everything
except the intense
Small talk forgotten
the second we stop talking

But when you fell
inside yourself
stunned to learn your own depth
When you wanted to
get to the top so bad
you leapt the middle steps
When you were always
one hell of a wreck
and being scared
brought out your best
and you remained
ahead of the game

That
I'll never forget

Seems like your maelstrom
has passed, let you relax
All those swirling sands
settled back to land
Glad as I am
I gotta admit
it makes me lonely

My life is still a cyclone and
it gets scary when it throws me

STRONG ROOTS

A thumbnail moon hangs witness
to verses nurtured during light
Whispered to gauge their power
into the fabric of the night

I find the spot
where the most crickets
chirp their mirth
The perfect thing to center me
and dissolve me into words

Surrounded by trees I envy
They know the benefits
of having strong roots
Beneath a sky a few shades darker
than the angry blue
of my latest bruise

I still see shapes
in long snuffed fires
our illusions dangling from branches
Hear leaves crushed into dust
by echoes left behind us

I should say goodnight to all this
Solidify lines on my way to the house
Hoping each isn't
the last I will find here
Someone put up signs here
I'm not allowed to seek them out

So thanks thumbnail moon
for your vigil
Rest well soot and cinder
Have fun you innocent echoes
Our naivete is with you
Goodnight arrogant trees
So certain no force can uproot you
Keep our illusions insulated
from the lightning
should it strike you
Thank you thumbnail moon
Tomorrow night
hang full near my window
Light the path for the echoes
from the forest to my pillow

BRICK BY BRICK

If Hell can freeze over, can Heaven catch fire?
I ask because my hell froze.
Now I fear its full force shrieking
after the blessings all around me.
All the things I find my heaven in
and try to add to, brick by brick

(Metaphorical brick, of course. In Heaven,
nothing as heavy as a brick would be tolerated)

But to the point; it's a heaven I'll protect

Fire by its nature is not some ancient evil
The monster that makes us fear it
is not its rightful owner
The monster's greatest weakness
is that its source of strength
is still just stolen property
which will one day be reclaimed

(Which means that if fire reached Heaven, Heaven would burn
the fire)

THE CURRENT

I've created things today
from skeletons and raw material
the current didn't take
I can beat the need for sleep back
I can always stay awake
to pull things from the flow
moving quick and invisible
in this or any place

I'd let you feel my thoughts
when they meander at pleasant paces
Not cold enough to end you
or superheated so they scald you
Not so fast they scare us both
'cos we can't tell where they're headed
Not so fast they hospitalize you
if you hit the rocks below them

But if you ask what my philosophy is
All I've salvaged amounts to this:

Pry the lid off of
your bug jar existence
When your captors dream
of righteousness
Feel your metamorphosis

BABY, I KNOW

I know, I know.
Baby, I know.
You always go crazy in private.
It's alright, it's alright.
Ok? It's alright.
But next time, please invite me.

LOVE IS OURS

Love is ours, among the huddled, wisecracking masses
Giving our increasingly uncharitable opinions
to the bitter cold wind that brittles them
and strikes them from the record

We're not on the clock right now, we really needn't worry
It's ok to be flesh and blood right now; forms of life
framing thoughts
against the company's best interest
Laughing all we can at the very concept's ridiculousness

Anyone having a boss, anyone *being* a boss
Anyone thinking they're in charge of anyone they can piss on
You can't do it without pissing them off unless
you get consent first

That's not necessarily what I'm here for, for I know love is ours
Even if you don't laugh like I do when the ass kissers call the
boss "Boss"

Now the store has got a sexism department
and courses on intimidating poses
Booksellers, no no no, we're a branch of the armed forces
I'll see your dosed up regulars and raise you
militantly gouging them

The best thing about the member card is
anywhere you shove it you'll fucking like it
The flavor explosion of lacquered plastic
will smash your whole damn palate

Seriously, though, love is ours, yours and mine but not the store's
Just because it's a reason why I haven't blown up the premises
is in no way meant to imply it belongs to the home office

Love is *ours ours ours*, I'll put it back if you delete it
Don't go in when your cig is done
stay out here and get me heated

NO INTENTION

Boys too smooth to sweat or bleed
Boys who come with no intention of staying
Striking boys I'd let strike more than twice

Flicker and gone
Boys will be boys

Boys who take my cigarettes and go
Who don't let me ride in exchange for a smoke

Vulgar boys who can't spell
Pretty boys who can't think
Who make me think up all kinds of scenarios for them

Boys in threadbare jeans behind five o'clock shadows
Taking mere minutes to tear me up
Taking seconds kicking shreds into darkness

Boys who run all ribboned in the sparky spectrum
of all I dare covet

Gifted boys
Boys who are gifts
Boys with presence long after unwrapping

BITE DOWN

Eyesight blurring, stomach churning
Always alone when I'm (always) worried
Overcaffeinated, effectively alienated
Ahead of the curve that
writes me off as outdated

Every glimpse I get of you with
that sharp smile blinging
I wonder who you are beneath
the quick defenses you build from everything

If I found you, If I lifted you
higher than me
Would you fight on, would you
bite down on me

Whatever branching dark canopy
the layers of years may shroud you with
I see your secret wilderness
No such animal as shame in it

I wonder where your hideout is and
how often the password changes
and my odds of being
sniped on sight
approaching with
my white flag waving

Deprived of sleep, essential vigilance
of unique freaks
Bitter, bitch you bet
but secretly (sporadically) sweet
I unveil such intel only
to bad boys who deserve a treat

Shall I expound on
sensation better shown than explained
I want out of this mind
into your veins
Surely there's freedom in going insane

LUCKY ONCE

In the disparity between what is and what's real
Between what I admit and what I conceal
I catalogue fully my culpability
in every crime I committed or abetted
and how I petitioned tribunals to triple my penance
So yes I did my time
though you weren't there to see it
and you think nothing's real unless you're a witness
and yes I fucking love you
You oblivious genius
I love you so much right now I just wanna smash things
Because I've never kissed you except those times I was sleeping
Odds are I won't get to 'cos goners aren't lucky
But I testify true
I was lucky once
I was on the run with the lucky ones
Damn what the lucky won
and lost to loathsomeness
pre-goner era
It left me wondering if once was my quota
If I luck out again the whole sky might fold inward
If the whole sky folded inward
then would you kiss me
If everything was ending could we finally start something
I need to know now that I've seen your eyes
They bat cliches new again
They chamber cool fire
Do holes in your vision kiss my reflection
or is that really me there
in your eyes swimming

or behind your eyes drowning
No longer protesting
The fight going out of me
Help isn't coming

THICK SOUTHERN

Auditory hallucinations ricocheting

More corporeal with every near miss

Tethered to touchstones

Most loved friend in mixed company

Cursory judgment sudden and jarring

More indisputable with each incorrect utterance

Relegated to roleplay

Unparalleled in creativity

Herky-jerk hedonism with a thick southern accent

An attention span never seemed so erotic

Is what seems retro really retro or outre

I disagree with what I'm forgetting I mean

ME WINNING YOU

Should be me winning you
Wrangling your top ten
treasures coveted
to surprise sexy smiles from
a dangerous angel

(The peasants gasp "Daaaang!"
Flocks upon flocks of
all kinds of F-bombs)

Laid out in time
for breakfast in bed
Wrapped and arranged
for maximum mileage
out of heart strum and cheek blush
Prizes poignant but problematic
to prudes with attitudinal certitude
Canceling any passion
for eroticized oppression
Poor bastards most brutalized
barred from fantasy especially

(Hell, hoodrat, back on track
This hood's lap is hip
He's too hot for politics)

Resolved to be a Romeo for
a whole new kind of lover
flipping from paradigm to paradigm

Sex sanguine and esoteric
while luxuriating unhurriedly

A hatefuck orgy of who all
we hide from each other
(Briefly
Barely
Bitter
Belligerent)

Gaping out our shamelessness
A thrust and jab shellacking

(Superpowers surge
Well-mannered
Pornographic)

DON'T BE AFRAID

Don't bring your beard to the movies with us
Don't be afraid of the movies
I'll be on good behavior
My very best behavior
The very best behavior
anyone's seen or will ever see

"Hey there, business major,
let's do business, I've got a list here,"
is only one of many things
I'd never dream of saying

CRAVING CONJURES

The treasure box is desolate
You invited but he doesn't come in
There's no pride in the pain anymore
Humor tries but the joke just hangs there

The neighborhood fog is a sudden barbed blanket
Anything could come from anywhere
except that one thing your craving bids you conjure
There's no luck in the love anymore
A parade jangles by
It stops you in place but it's not in your honor

The bed is not your bed anymore
He fell asleep there once and that makes it his
There's no peace anyplace anymore
He stood on that porch before
He shops at that store

So try humor try
but the treasure's been lifted
Because I can't forget it I must walk in the fog
Let it take me anywhere
Take from me anything
Until craving conjures and he comes parading in

TENDON AND BLOOD

A life spent tracking clarity
Such a timid fox
Showing its face only briefly
Only in the absence of love

If I caught it would I kill it
to divine a future from tendon and blood
A fruitless endeavor anyway
since secrets are something I've loved

There's some inherent mystery
in the way your name tastes on my tongue

If all is revealed
in a foxhole by torchlight
Will I divine a future
as antiseptic as the past

These windows
however spotless
are only earthly glass

Is it all the same lesson
Forever look but don't touch
I found what I've been missing
Even that cuts

The same sting as yearning
Every inch as deep as persecution
or the dark irony of witch hunts
organized by witches

DANCE BOY DANCE BOY

Kiss them kiss them kiss them all
Dance boy dance boy grind and paw
There's one there's one just one you really want
Fuck him fuck him or it doesn't matter who you fuck
Roll with it roll with it the party never ends
We'll die one day we'll die one day they'll hire our replacements
They can't be us they can't be us they'll pride themselves and preen
Our mark is made our mark is made it returns after washing
I'm happy now I'm happy now I wouldn't tell a lie
I'm nothing now I'm nothing now so I'm easily satisfied

SEND FOR ME

Cripple me to see if it feels any different
Trick me out of fortunes to fortify your dissonance
The ripple effect of your disaffected swagger
might trip me into ditches
Mindfuck me ragged

I'm generous of soul but that's not why your hand's out
You're harmful to my heart
You benefit from doubt

If you're all up in my space why can't I touch your face
You war on my brain relentlessly
'til I think of it as my peace

So send for me a dozen times a day
just to reiterate that you sent me away
and I don't even have enough guile to make you sorry
because I fell and now there's not an iota
of willful defiance in my being
to make you regret how unbelievably
unendingly
wrong you are about me

Now the moment I never make you wait for
where I contradict myself completely

Regret not
Regret us not
Regret is not what I'm bringing you

The call and response
The resonance cuts
Recall the reasons for ringing me

GREAT BIG WORLD

I do love you
(not that you believe or care)

I remember your careless orbit
(how it centered me, how I chased it)

I don't expect you'll call back
(you won't remember)

It's a great big world out there
(infinite space beyond it)

Endlessness within me
(you ended us without me)

My new apartment's a dive but I toast it with wine
(because it's sort of mine, sort of, just like you were)

I think I make enough to keep it but it's harder to be sure now
(you're just a little shit who vanished with so much of my value)

The place is shrinking
(or else I'm shrinking)

or the great big world's shrinking
(or infinite space is shrinking)

I'm staring at reality shrinking
(for the first time I'm blinking)

SAVAGE ANTHEM

You hum and it hears

my hollow hungry ache

to feed your savage anthem

Put my head between your teeth

Nourish your mighty chorus

SUCH POTENTIAL

Feel unchained, metaphorically
bloodstained
"Let there be light"
references your eyes
A breath
A scent
A touch
Unless we got to write it let's not
do this by the book
Go ahead, be pretentious
Not desolate
Sweat gives me away
Your glance refracts
gunning me down stunningly
'til I just can't fight the power
You steady your aim
then fire and fire
Smash me into gibberish
before the eclipse
Stretch out in horizontal lounge
Conquer my entire horizon
Snowdrift shivers
Mushroom cloud of
Invisible, silent colors
Such potential
Entwine grapevine fingers
Comic book sound effects
to announce a big entrance
Catastrophe
hitting notes of tragedy

to make you marrow
Liquor waiting, growing rank
Awaiting unjamming of
body shot traffic

MY TURN

Dust to ashes, ashes to dust
I say that because I'm not who I was
Ever since I scoured the rust
Can't help but feel no one feels very much

Unless it relates to drugs

What I ask from you is no more than I give to you
but I do not live in you, so I must live in spite of you
and the sad shadow that shrouds you
where love's light once found you
and lit you from within

I can't keep letting you win

Photos, carvings, names scrawled on my dresser
Campfires burning through the whims of the weather
Moments where each of you
helped make something better
Concessions I made that you never remember

More often than not, I wish I didn't either

Whatever I took from you
I thought freely given
How fine did you print your terms and conditions

Now it's my turn to make restrictions

FRAGILE/PROBLEMATIC

Why believe my truth
When his lie is more dramatic
Why feel like I was used
when his lie is less traumatic
We fell too far too soon
Our stubborn natures were problematic
and the moment he could mark me fragile
he left me broken in the attic

UNDER WRAPS

"For now, we can talk," you said
My heart heard and sang
My mind stopped doom scrolling
The future brightened again

We can talk about whatever you like
Just please give me some of your time
to stun with sweet schemes to cherish you
in deed, in word, in rhyme

I need you, in fact, I have for a while
I hope that's ok to say
'cos my mood swings unpredictably
with the pain of being away

I'll keep my proposal under wraps
You'd scoff "Too soon! Too much!"
but part of me's still asking you
anytime I feel your touch

Sometimes I get pretentious
but with you, I try to refrain
Some truths are really simple:
I'm devoted to you every day

Everything it's too soon for
I've anticipated for years
I've been waiting, if not patiently,
devoutly and sincere

The love I feel is real
It's a prayer I recite when I kneel
The God in me knows the God in you
No pleasure is a sin to unveil

My freedom can find and free you
My soul sees you as hope
Whatever happens, I'll side with you
Wherever I am, you have a home

STAY HAUNTED

I'm not terrified
by a haunting I wouldn't exorcize
You left yourself here
Persistent poltergeist
Upending every furnishing
and fixture resembling sense

So walk right through
if that's the only way I'll mix with you
If that's the touch we'll share
however brief
I will stay haunted
I'll cry in my sleep

Dreaming of a better reality
Waking to a reality
that would make a dismal dream

I'm not sorry
for molten secrets bubbled from my core
I couldn't keep them
Couldn't blister anymore
Charred inside, outward cold
The inevitability of eruption

So burn me down
if it's the only taste of heat you'll allow
If it's your burning urge
However brief
I will blister again
I'll melt in my sleep

Dreaming of the original torch
Enough light to see by
Kept close to me for warmth

WHEN YOU LAND

Stained windows smashed
Colored glass
Colors the world
when light refracts

I think you're
the missing shard in the picture

All the dead ends self-imposed
You cuff the stirring
sunk in your soul
Sometimes you're the only one
who can't see how you've grown
Even then you're the only one
who knows the things you know

I think you
should learn to think bigger

Skies that open
over tides
Through seasons
There are sharks in the oceans
but love's made on beaches

Can I be the sand you'll be wearing
Will you be a comet I can watch
There
then fading

Atmosphere trailing
Gone from the eyes
Burned into the thoughts

I think when you land
I should be there

BEST GUESS

I try to make people laugh
because I can't stand
seeing anyone cry

I try to make people cry
so I can admit
the deadliness of life

I try to drag into the light
truths people wouldn't
be caught dead telling

One day I'll outfeel intellect
One day
I'll outreason rebellion

Maybe today
but
probably not

I'm a defeatist
but
I'll take my best shot

I'm no elitist
so I should bring
my second best

Who gives a fuck
I just try
to impress

Because you might not be love
but
you are my best guess

Why I laugh
when I'm sad
like Alanis Morissette

Why my karma
brings cops
like Radiohead

Why life is
too damn short
not to pounce despite all doubt

As Mr. Cobain's
brutal brilliance
will eternally point out

I FORGET ME

When you forget me
I forget me too
When I forget me
I still remember you

ABOUT ATMOSPHERE PRESS

Atmosphere Press is an independent, full-service publisher for excellent books in all genres and for all audiences. Learn more about what we do at atmospherepress.com.

We encourage you to check out some of Atmosphere's latest releases, which are available at Amazon.com and via order from your local bookstore:

Melody in Exile, by S.T. Grant

Covenant, by Kate Carter

Near Scattered Praise Lies Our Substantial Endeavor, by Ron Penoyer

Weightless, Woven Words, by Umar Siddiqui

Journeying: Flying, Family, Foraging, by Nicholas Ranson

Lexicon of the Body, by DM Wallace

Controlling Chaos, by Michael Estabrook

Almost a Memoir, by M.C. Rydel

Throwing the Bones, by Caitlin Jackson

Like Fire and Ice, by Eli

Sway, by Tricia Johnson

A Patient Hunger, by Skip Renker

Lies of an Indispensable Nation: Poems About the American Invasions of Iraq and Afghanistan, by Lilvia Soto

The Carcass Undressed, by Linda Eguiliz

Poems That Wrote Me, by Karissa Whitson

Gnostic Triptych, by Elder Gideon

For the Moment, by Charnjit Gill

Battle Cry, by Jennifer Sara Widelitz

I woke up to words today, by Daniella Deutsch

Never Enough, by William Guest

Second Adolescence, by Joe Rolnicki

ABOUT THE AUTHOR

TRAVIS HUPP lives in the Shenadoah Valley of Virginia. When he's not writing, he's usually getting outsmarted by his 16-year-old Pomeranian, Oz, and his 10-year-old terrier, Willow, who have decided to ask for forgiveness instead of permission. *Faster, Annihilators!* is his first published work.